GOOD ✦ OLD ✦ DAYS®

Live It Again™
1952

Dear Friends,

1952 was a year filled with growth and prosperity. Young couples of all backgrounds demonstrated great optimism in their personal lives. We married and became parents at a rate previously unseen. With the explosion of families came a bounty of new housing construction, mostly built in the sprawling suburbs. It didn't matter if your house looked the same as your neighbor's residence, it was yours and it was home.

Suburban life also made automobiles more of a necessity as men commuted to their jobs and women relied on cars to do their shopping and transport the children to events. Cars also became the central feature of teen culture. Remember your first car, that dream machine with the powerful V8 engine, gleaming chrome and soaring fins? Automobiles of 1952 were not just basic transportation, but also symbolized freedom and individuality.

Television was in the midst of a golden age of fantastic growth. Every family longed for "that piece of furniture that stares back at you," as Bob Hope called it. We purchased TVs by the thousand, and watching our favorite shows became part of the weekly routine. We invited Lucille Ball, star of *I Love Lucy*, into our living rooms and laughed at her wacky antics. We were thrilled with the plots and action on the detective show, *Dragnet*. We were charmed by the box with the flickering tube.

> **"Automobiles . . . symbolized freedom and individuality."**

Heroic World War II general, Dwight D. Eisenhower, was overwhelmingly chosen as the Republican candidate for president. With his grandfatherly grin and affable personality, slogan writers came up with mottos such as "I Like Ike", which were printed on signs and attached to campaign buttons. We did indeed like Ike, turning out on Election Day to give him a landslide victory.

1952 was also a shining year for sports as the Olympic Games took center stage. The winter Olympics, held in Oslo, Norway, propelled American figure skater Dick Button into the spotlight as he successfully performed the first triple loop in competition. At the summer games in Helsinki, Finland, we cheered as we watched the United States defeat the Soviet Union for the basketball gold medal.

As you turn the pages of this nostalgia book, enjoy your cruise back to 1952. May the vista in the rearview mirror of your life bring back many pleasant memories. See you on down the road.

Contents

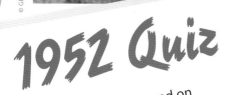

REPRINTED WITH PERMISSION FROM FORD MOTOR COMPANY

© GETTY IMAGES

1952 Quiz

1. What famous couple wed on March 4, 1952?

2. What was the last name of the family who starred in the TV show *The Adventures of Ozzie & Harriet*?

3. Name the No. 1 TV show in 1952.

4. Who was Dwight D. Eisenhower's running mate in the 1952 presidential election?

5. Where were the 1952 Winter Olympics held?

6. Who won the 1952 Indianapolis 500 race?

7. Who sang the 1952 No. 1 song, "Wheel of Fortune"?

Answers appear on page 127

© GETTY IMAGES

COURTESY OF CHRYSLER GROUP LLC

New RCA Victor TVs were advertised as having a "magic monitor," with reception that adjusted automatically.

Young and old alike took a break from work and shopping to get a glimpse of the new televisions.

Sylvania TVs also came with an AM-FM radio and a three-speed record player.

Westinghouse advertised a picture so real, you live the action.

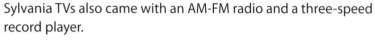

The Metro Daily News

FINAL EDITION

THE WEATHER
City and Suburbs—Rain.
Snow, Colder.

VOLUME 30 — No. 104   20 PAGES   FIVE CENTS

JANUARY 14, 1952

TODAY PREMIERES ON NBC WITH DAVE GARROWAY AS HOST

This news show becomes one of the longest-running television series in America.

Television

Our first TV

Televisions were found in an increasing number of homes, reaching 17 million by the end of 1952. America's first television generation formed the habit of passing many after-school hours being entertained by their favorite programs. Most Americans didn't want to miss one minute of their favorite shows. Television stars often portrayed an idealized version of American families where problems were solved more quickly and easily than in real life. The television revolution caused significant changes in daily lifestyles. Viewers tended to stay up later at night and leave home less often. Restaurants were more crowded during early evening hours so people could get back to the "tube" for the evening shows.

Sparton's Cosmic Eye televisions were promoted as having a picture so clear, "it's like having an eye in the sky."

Emerson TVs led the field in performance with the lowest price of all, starting at $180.

Motorola televisions were the standard for fine furniture styling in television. The window shoppers at the top of page 6 became enthusiastic buyers.

Television

Shows premiering in 1952

In the early 1950s, Americans thought they were satisfied with their ritual of breakfast, coffee and the morning paper. Then in January 1952, NBC gave them an alternative: a live version of the daily news, called *Today*. Audio news streamed in from Washington, D.C., London and Germany while a remote camera in Chicago showed commuters. The *Adventures of Superman*, first aired in 1952, boasted imaginative story lines and color before most people had color TV sets. *The Adventures of Ozzie & Harriet* starred the real life Nelson family. The series attracted large audiences and although it was never a top-ten hit, it became synonymous with ideal American family life.

For millions of kids, actor George Reeves *was* superman. He starred along with Phyllis Coats as Lois Lane in the television series *Adventures of Superman*.

Men drive a mule team for the television show, *Death Valley Days*. It was a series featuring true stories of the old American West, introduced by host, Stanley Andrews.

The Nelsons—Ozzie, Harriet, David and Ricky—became one of America's favorite TV families.

Filming a show in ABC's New York television studio, a converted riding school.

Television Shows Debuting in 1952

Today

Death Valley Days

I've Got a Secret

The Guiding Light

This Is the Life

Adventures of Superman

Victory at Sea

American Bandstand

Life Is Worth Living

My Little Margie

See It Now

Adventures of Ozzie & Harriet

The Ernie Kovacs Show

Meet the Masters

This is Your Life

Life With Elizabeth

Estelle Parsons was the *Today* show's first Today Girl, whose responsibilities included filling in the weather and temperature.

Tops on Television

I Love Lucy
CBS

Arthur Godfrey's Talent Scouts
CBS

Arthur Godfrey and His Friends
CBS

Dragnet
NBC

Texaco Star Theater
NBC

The Buick Circus Hour
NBC

The Colgate Comedy Hour
NBC

Gangbusters
NBC

You Bet Your Life
NBC

Fireside Theater
NBC

Dean Martin and Jerry Lewis clown around in a Hollywood studio. The image on the monitor is the same one seen by the cameraman.

Actors Vivian Vance, Lucille Ball, William Frawley and Desi Arnaz defend their living room against invaders in an episode of the television series *I Love Lucy*. Each week the whole crew brought much laughter into our homes.

Television

Our favorite shows

The *I Love Lucy* show had become a fixture in the homes of Americans. As Lucy Ricardo, actress Lucille Ball perfected her scatterbrained act and loud crying fits when things weren't going her way. Audiences empathized with and adored her. Variety hour shows *Arthur Godfrey and His Friends* and companion show, *Arthur Godfrey's Talent Scouts*, shot to near the top of the ratings. Part of the appeal was in Godfrey's repertory company of singers, all of them good clean kids who had been lifted out of obscurity. TV detective Joe Friday, played by Jack Webb, kept the streets of Los Angeles safe in the highly successful show *Dragnet*. It depicted cases taken from actual police files, changing the participants' names "to protect the innocent."

Musician and television host Arthur Godfrey outspreads his arms as he sits on a chair and holds his trademark ukulele during an episode of his CBS variety program, *Arthur Godfrey and His Friends.*

Actor Roy Rogers and his wife, actress Dale Evans, made films for TV at their California ranch.

FAMOUS BIRTHDAYS
Walter Mosley, January 12
author
Teddy Gentry, January 22
bass guitarist (Alabama)

What Made Us Laugh

"We didn't take any pictures on our vacation this time, so we'll just show you last year's again."

"I interrupt this program to bring you a special weather bulletin!"

"It's not that he's so heavy, Daddy. You're standing on his skis."

"Okay now, put some beef in this one."

"Anything catch your fancy?"

"Mom, the Smiths are moving!"

"Why, yes … I'd like a demonstration."

"My report card—and I'm tired of
watching television anyway."

Winter Fun

The winter season brought falling temperatures and, in many parts of the country, snow. A bountiful supply of white flakes was especially welcomed by children. When the temperature was just right and snow packed well, the variety of activities was endless. Making snowmen invariably ended with snowball fights. Well-bundled children hid behind snow forts and stockpiled snowballs in preparation for all-out wars. Ice skating was also enjoyed during the winter months, but required more equipment and finesse. Skating required strong ankles and first experiences were usually filled with plenty of bottom-first encounters with slick, cold ice. Those who lived near hills and mountains enjoyed brisk afternoons filled with sledding and skiing.

© 1952 SEPS

A couple twirls around the ice holding hands during an afternoon date.

A neighbor's pond is converted into a skating rink where adults and children alike sharpen their skating skills.

JOHN FALTER

FAMOUS BIRTHDAYS
Randy Forbes, February 17
politician
Sharon Dahlonega Raiford Bush, February 29 primetime
weather anchor

Bonfires were occasionally built near the skiing and sledding hills to serve as warming stations.

Making snowmen became a competition of who could create the most unique specimen.

Few things are as invigorating as a well-aimed snowball to the face.

Eigil Nansen, grandson of famous explorer Fridtjob Nansen, carries the torch on the final leg. A flame was lit in the hearth of the home of Sondre Nordheim, who had done much to popularize skiing, and relayed by 94 skiers to Oslo, Norway.

Winter Olympics

Oslo, Norway

The Olympic Games finally came to Norway, the birthplace of modern skiing. A new hotel was built for the press and dignitaries. Three buildings were converted for athletes and coaches. Host nation Norway won the most medals with a total of 16. Norwegian speed skater Hjalmar Andersen won three gold medals, the largest total for any athlete at the games. Germany regained its former bobsleigh glory with wins in both the four- and two-man events. American figure skater Richard "Dick" Button only needed to perform a safe program to retain his Olympic title. Instead, he chose to attempt a triple loop, even though no skater had ever performed it in competition, and claimed his second gold medal.

Dick Button of the United States, reigning world champion figure skater, defends his Olympic title while performing the "Flying Splits."

The official poster for the 1952 Winter Olympic games. Thirty countries and 693 athletes participated.

Winter Olympics
Athletes in action

American skier Andrea Mead Lawrence was known for her focus and determination. She easily won her first Olympic gold medal on the opening day. She crashed on the first run of her next race, but managed to ski perfectly for the second run to win her second gold medal.

A record number of 150,000 people gather at Holmenkollen Hill to watch the ski jumping competition on the last day of the games. Most attended to cheer on host Norway's athletes. The Norwegian athletes did not disappoint the crowd, winning gold and silver medals.

The Canadian hockey team, favored to win the gold medal, played the United States to a 3-3 tie at the gold medal game. Based on the international rules, the gold medal was given to Canada and the United States received the silver medal. The teams from Canada and the United States were criticized for their rough play. While body checking was legal, it was not often used by European teams. Opponents and spectators held a dim view of this style of play.

The American women's Olympic ski team members left to right: Betty Weir, Jeannette Burr, Imogene Opton, Katy Rodolph, Sally Neidlinger, Gretchen Fraser, Sandra Tomlinson and Andrea Mead Lawrence.

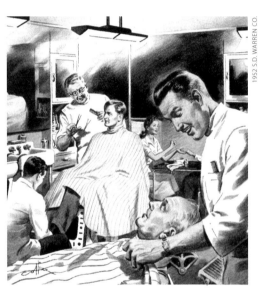

Hairdressers were often the source for the latest in community news.

Barbershops were also a place for men to socialize.

A family shops for a new pet.

Service station attendants usually pumped a buck's worth, but occasionally customers would say, "Five dollars or fill, whichever comes first."

Neighborhood Shops

In 1952, many shops still provided personalized service. Men went to the barbershop for more than haircuts; they also enjoyed the male camaraderie. Women frequented beauty shops to receive a cut and style while catching up on the latest news. Main Street, lined with small stores, was still the place to shop. Afternoons were spent window shopping for everything from a new pet to the latest in fashion. Customer service was a key factor in the success of any local gas station. Attendants also washed windows, checked the oil and battery, and filled tires as needed. Ice-cream stands were popular stops to cap off a shopping trip.

Ice cream tasted better when it didn't come wrapped in plastic and was served with a smile.

Though chain stores were beginning to make their mark on the shopping experience, many preferred to visit the local grocer who knew patrons and their children on a first-name basis.

At the Office

The Sensimatic machine was able to perform many business functions semi-automatically. It had a moving programmable carriage to maintain ledgers.

Victor's new Super-Quiet Customs adding machines could also subtract, multiply, divide and calculate.

The modern office of 1952 included machines that increased productivity as well as reduced noise and operator fatigue. Electric typewriters and adding machines were faster, easier to operate and quiet as a whisper. Even the smallest office could afford the convenience and prestige of metered mail with a postage meter. Despite the media stereotype of the stay-at-home lady, the numbers of working women, though mainly secretarial and clerical jobs, increased throughout 1952. The career woman wore tailored wool suits over silk blouses, also donning gloves and a hat. Men spent a large portion of their income on suits, hats, overcoats, and briefcases in order to meet corporate expectations. In fact, it was not uncommon to spend a week's salary on one new suit.

"If your secretary wants a postage meter, she has your best interest at heart. A postage meter saves time and work, and usually postage."

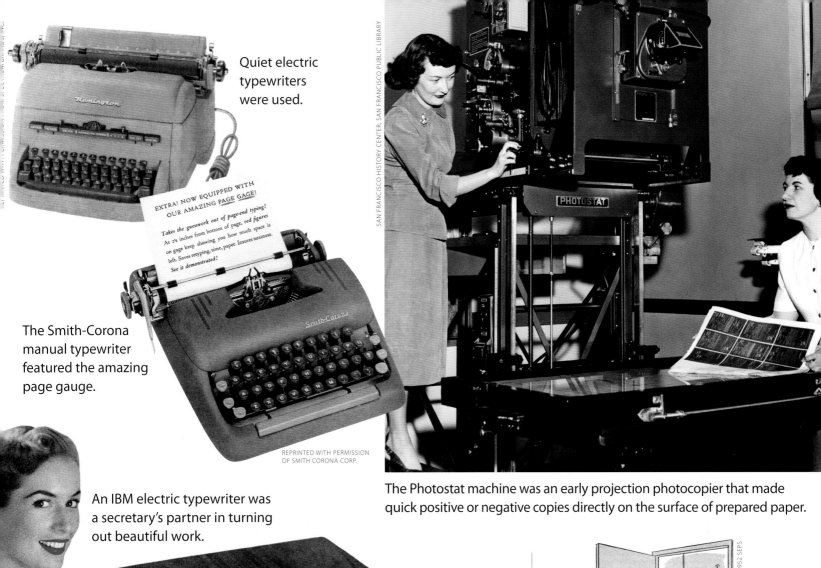

Quiet electric typewriters were used.

The Smith-Corona manual typewriter featured the amazing page gauge.

An IBM electric typewriter was a secretary's partner in turning out beautiful work.

The Photostat machine was an early projection photocopier that made quick positive or negative copies directly on the surface of prepared paper.

"I found those Johnson papers here in my desk drawer but I haven't the nerve to go out and tell them."

General Motors factory engineers inspect parts to locate those in need of further improvement.

Construction workers had plenty of work keeping up with the demand for new housing.

Gas station attendants pumped gas, along with cleaning the windshield and checking the radiator, battery and tires.

A businessman's wife drives him to the train station to catch the commuter train to work. He returns rumpled and tired, but successful.

Men at Work

Large numbers of Americans enjoyed prosperity in 1952. It was a time of relatively low unemployment and high wages with an average yearly salary of $3,658. The construction boom of post-World War II stimulated the economy. Most jobs were in the areas of industry, agriculture and construction. Basic industries such as automotive, steel and oil flourished. As businesses expanded, more Americans were able to move from blue-collar jobs on the shop floor or assembly line to white-collar jobs as managers or technicians. Many Americans who worked in factories and shops were now able to enjoy a middle-class lifestyle, which included home ownership, a decent car and enough money left over for vacations, college and retirement. People expected to hold down one job their entire lives and retire at age 62.

These men are taking a break to find out what the score is during the World Series. Working with power lines required men who were steady-handed and comfortable with heights.

Dump-truck drivers did their part to construct roads by hauling away large rocks and bringing in gravel.

THE WEATHER

The Metro Daily News

FINAL EDITION

FEBRUARY 21, 1952

LIZ TAYLOR MARRIES MICHAEL WILDING

This is Liz's second marriage.

Men at Work

The price of progress

When Dwight D. Eisenhower was elected President in November, 1952, the Bureau of Public Roads admitted that 76 percent of roads were inadequate. Even the best rural highways were narrow two-lane roads. The push for a new highway system was promoted as a matter of national security if nuclear war erupted. New turnpikes, expressways and superhighways with overpasses and underpasses were built. More land was required for the ever-widening and lengthening roads. Land was also needed for pipe lines to more effectively distribute natural gas and oil. Progress did not come without a certain amount of sacrifice. Under eminent domain, some landowners were required to give up property in exchange for fair market value.

Built to high design standards imposed by the federal government, the new interstate system came with a price tag of $50 billion.

Farm fields were replaced with large earth-moving machines to create the American road network of over three million miles.

Gas pipe lines
are laid through
property acquired
by eminent domain.

Pipe lines brought
natural gas and oil
in greater volume
to more users.

A house is moved to another location to make way
for a new road.

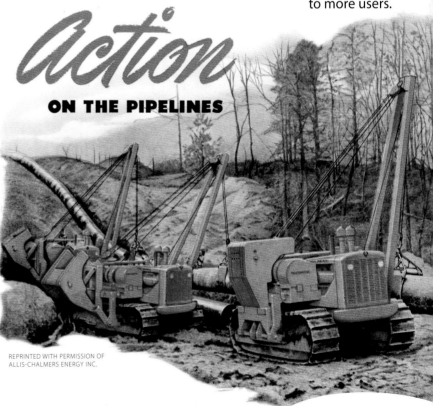

Action

ON THE PIPELINES

REPRINTED WITH PERMISSION OF
ALLIS-CHALMERS ENERGY INC.

A popular 35mm camera, the Argus C3, had every feature a photographer could want for $69.

IT'S NEW!

SHOWS YOUR PICTURE*
BEFORE YOU TAKE IT!

*It's a brilliant full-size preview! (2¼ x 2¼).

The new Graflex 22 camera was easy to use with the ability to view the entire picture before it was taken. There was no longer any excuse for cut-off heads or tilted photos, and the camera only cost $89.

JOHN FALTER

Family photos taken by professional photographers were cherished.

Slide projectors displayed slides in brilliant, true color; the perfect companion for a 35mm camera.

Captured Moments

The baby boom, combined with the growing affluence of millions of middle-class Americans, helped spur the sale of portable motion-picture cameras so families could chronicle their lives. By 1952, 8mm home-movie cameras were a common sight at family parties, special events and on vacations. For the family photo album, there were more choices when buying cameras with prices ranging from $15 to $90. Kodak's Brownie 127 was the top-selling model, emphasizing simplicity as a point-and-shoot camera. The Brownie popularized low-cost photography and introduced the concept of the snapshot. For those with more cash to spend and a passion for photography, there were 35mm cameras that took photos in black-and-white, action, flash and gorgeous color.

"It's high speed—I even caught Lucy with her mouth closed."

Bell and Howell's 8mm home-movie projector was advertised for $100 and guaranteed for life.

Anyone could operate a movie camera with the new lightweight designs.

© 1952 SEPS

Fathers wanted their daughters to marry well and weren't above occasional matchmaking.

Love Is in the Air

The courtship

When dating, couples converged on soda shops, restaurants and drive-ins. Although eating was an essential activity at these gathering places, the quality of the food was definitely secondary. The point was to get together, flirt, show off a little and chat. Many couples met at the drive-in theater. Upon arriving, a carload of friends would cruise slowly around to see who was already there, and then begin to circulate from car to car. If a couple was "going steady," they were expected to remain loyal to one another. Friendship rings, charms and pins were visible signs of commitment. Swimming, biking, hiking, watching television, skiing and skating were all possibilities for dating fun.

Dining out could become an education in international food, especially when chopsticks were used instead of silverware.

© 1952 SEPS

Hot weather, double dates and swimming were a winning combination for summer fun.

"That's the director. He likes to play a small part in all of his pictures."

Dating fun could be found at home as well, like this couple singing a duet at the piano.

Couples could find private time to get to know one another by going for long walks.

Love Is in the Air

Tying the knot

Postwar prosperity allowed many brides to experience a full-fledged traditional wedding with all the trimmings. Catered weddings, engraved invitations and wedding photographers all became fixtures of the milestone event. Wedding gowns had fitted bodices and very full skirts. Made of elegant materials, such as silk organza and lace, the dresses had petticoats to create a billowy bell shape. Wedding veils were almost universal, but very few gowns had trains. Popular wedding colors were pastel pinks and blues, with pink peonies as the top choice in flowers. There were fewer clothing options for the groom, who usually wore a basic black tuxedo.

The wedding-planning fun started after the diamond was placed on her finger.

A white wedding was the ultimate dream for an affluent, middle class bride.

Bridal showers were fun and made it easier for the bride to set up housekeeping in style.

"Is it washable?"

"It's a boy ... six feet two and weighing 190 pounds."

Dressed in traditional wedding clothes, the bride and groom repeat their vows and exchange rings. Couples tied the knot at a younger age. The average age for the groom was 23 and the bride was 20.

Tiaras like the one this bride is wearing were the trend.

The Metro Daily News

FINAL EDITION

FIVE CENTS

MARCH 4, 1952

ACTOR RONALD REAGAN AND ACTRESS NANCY DAVIS WED

Reagan later became the 33rd Governor of California from 1969 to 1975 and the 40th President of the United States from 1981 to 1989.

Our Homes

The baby boom was now in full force and families grew at amazing rates. Builders and developers could barely meet the demand for new housing. The result was the mass production of standardized middle-class homes in huge suburban tracts. The ranch house emerged as a popular icon, which was basically a one-story rectangle, with the long side facing the street, complete with a picture window. Most houses had a carport at one end to shelter the family car and no longer had front porches. Due to low cost and simplicity, the ranch house was the ideal starter home, allowing more Americans to become first-time homebuyers.

© 1952 SEPS

Everyone, it seemed, wanted to be a part of the post-war American Dream of owning their own home.

Inexpensive house plans abounded.

The Metro Daily News

THE WEATHER
City and State—Rain,
Snow, Colder

VOLUME 87 — No. 165

FINAL
EDITION

20 PAGES   FIVE CENTS

APRIL 30, 1952

MR. POTATO HEAD IS FIRST TOY ADVERTISED ON TELEVISION

Many homes featured open floor plans and the family room became a standard part of a typical house. Pink fixtures were frequently used in bathrooms and cheery red paint created the picture-book kitchen.

International Harvester offered refrigerators with a five-year warranty, extra door space and large freezers that defrosted automatically every night. The refrigerator was available with colorful door handles to match the kitchen's color scheme.

Owning an American Kitchens Roto-Tray dishwasher was like having a maid in the kitchen. For only nine cents a day, dishwashers pre-rinsed, washed, triple rinsed, dried and stored dishes.

General Electric advertised ranges with double ovens for $350.

Our Homes

Appliances make life easier

The postwar era promised new and wondrous appliances. Major manufacturers like Westinghouse, General Electric, Frigidaire and Whirlpool did their best to convince consumers it was time to modernize. Functionalism was stressed in these appliances, but they also included as much shiny chrome as possible. After eight years of secret research, American Kitchens advertised the most modern, work-free dishwasher ever developed. It had a rotating tray that assured spotlessly clean dishes. Refrigerators could be purchased in a rainbow of colors with sparkling trim. General Electric sold ranges for as low as $210 and manufactured washing machines for about $300. All this technology reduced the workload for women.

With General Electric's automatic washing machine, it was so easy to do the family wash. No more wringing out clothes by hand.

The woman in this advertisement is thrilled with her beautiful new White sewing machine. It featured forward and backward sewing and sold for about $85.

FAMOUS BIRTHDAYS
Annette O'Toole, April 1 actress
Mary McDonnell, April 28 actress

Our Homes

Mobile living

Originally, house trailers tended to be smaller units used for vacationing or for retired folks escaping cold winters by temporarily going south. But due to post-World War II housing shortages, larger versions were marketed as permanent homes. Even after the shortage subsided, trailer homes were still sold to thousands of low-income and alternative-living Americans, who considered them more convenient than apartments. Some trailers were enormous, ranging up to 50 feet in length and priced from $3,500 to as high as $25,000. For those whose jobs required frequent moves, mobile homes were the ideal choice. They simply took their home with them.

Mobile homes featured tiny living rooms, kitchens and bathrooms with all the conveniences of a standard house.

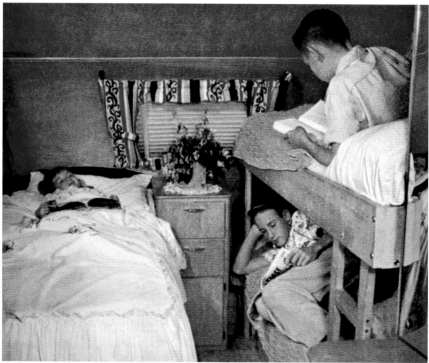

Children had their own bedroom in this house trailer, and bunk beds were built to make the most of the small space.

TRAILER PARK
OFFICE →

JOHN & LIZZIE
WILSON
BOSTON, MASS.

AV
E.

Actor George Burns and actress Gracie Allen dine at an upscale Hollywood restaurant.

Film actress Floria DeHaven, who starred in *Two Tickets to Broadway*, and her toy French poodle visit the swimming pool of a fancy Los Vegas hotel.

FAMOUS BIRTHDAYS
Beth Henley, May 8 actress
Mr. T, May 21 actor

Janet Leigh and her husband, Tony Curtis, enjoy a carefree moment at a swimming pool.

Stargazing Hollywood Style

Being a star wasn't entirely about enjoying life in the limelight. It also involved hard work and guarding against competitors. Teenagers drooled over movie stars Tony Curtis and Janet Leigh, who were thought of as two perfect specimens mated in paradise. They were married, despite protests from Tony's studio, whose executives feared he would ruin his box-office appeal. For twenty years, Bert Lahr was a top-money comedian but still feared he was a flop although he earned about $200,000 a year. George Burns and Gracie Allen were a comedy team and among the few who managed to achieve long-term success.

Comedian Bert Lahr's children play in their ten-room New York apartment. Bert is well known for his role as the Cowardly Lion in the *Wizard of Oz*.

Mona Freeman, popular teenage movie star of *The Greatest Show on Earth*, and Coleen Gray, who starred in the movie *Kansas City Confidential*, lunch at the Beverly Hills Derby.

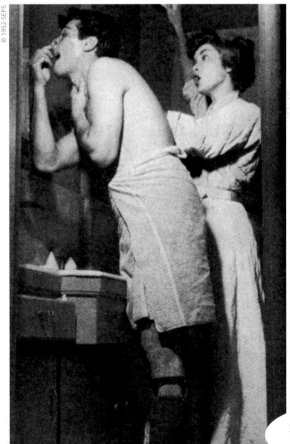

Janet Leigh and Tony Curtis get ready for work. There was only one bathroom in their Hollywood apartment.

President Harry S. Truman

There were many challenges for President Truman in 1952. The United States was mired in a war in Korea that promised no quick resolution. The war interfered with normal business operations. Citing a national wartime emergency, Truman ordered the government to seize steel mills that were about to close due to labor strikes. A polio epidemic was raging and cold war tensions intensified. The White House was found to be structurally unsound, and President Truman asked Congress for funding to rebuild it from the inside out, leaving only the brick outer walls. The President and his wife, Bess, resided across the street in Blair House and moved back to the White House on March 27, 1952.

President Truman gives an address at the Jefferson-Jackson Day Dinner on March 29, 1952. It is at this event that he announced he would not be a presidential candidate for the next election.

President Truman throws the first baseball at the 1952 opening game between the Washington Senators and the Boston Red Sox.

Official Navy portrait of President Harry S. Truman.

President Truman meets with the "Big Four" Congressional leaders. Left to right, standing: Senate Majority Leader Ernest McFarland and House Majority Leader John W McCormack; seated: Vice President Alben Barkley, President Truman and Speaker of the House Sam Rayborn.

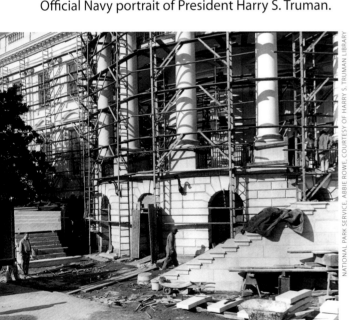

Though Bess Truman steadfastly fulfilled the social obligations of her position; she did not enjoy the lack of privacy.

New steps of the South Portico are being erected during the White House renovation. The White House reconstruction began in 1949 and ended in 1952.

Actor and film producer John Garfield reacts as he is questioned by the House Committee on Un-American Activities. This committee investigated Communist influence in the entertainment industry. Garfield testified that he is not and has never been a member of the Communist Party.

The four pilots in Goose Gay, Labrador, are photographed after completing the second leg of their historic transatlantic helicopter flight. They are: Capt. Vincent H. McGovern (left), Lt. Harold Moore, Capt. George Hambrick and Capt. Harry Jeffers.

The Metro Daily News

THE WEATHER
City off Showers-Rain.
Snow, Colder
Month & Rain Amount

FINAL EDITION

VOLUME 41 — No. 181

FIVE CENTS

MAY 8, 1952

OF THEE I SING OPENS AT ZIEGFELD THEATER

This show runs for 72 performances.

United States Events

In 1952, the world's first transatlantic helicopter crossing took place with a total flight time of about 52 hours. Despite extremist opposition, on July 25, 1952, Puerto Rico's new constitution was officially established. On this page is a Puerto Rican street filled with American Coca-Cola signs. Joseph McCarthy's reckless accusations against suspected communists gave the English language a new word, "McCarthyism." Though a few spies were found guilty and sentenced, some people had their careers and reputations ruined by allegations. On the lighter side of the news, Tony the Tiger was introduced as the cartoon mascot for Kellogg's Frosted Flakes and became a breakfast cereal icon.

Medical Advancement

President Truman was an outspoken supporter of federally funded medical research. A number of improvements were implemented for treatment of heart disorders. For the first time, a mechanical heart was used to sustain a patient during heart surgery. Also pioneered was the use of electric shock as a cardiac-arrest rescue technique. Facing an illness that could lead to paralysis or death made polio every parent's worst nightmare. The vaccine to protect against polio was developed in 1952 by Jonas Salk. Dr. Salk was hailed as a miracle worker and endeared himself to the public by refusing to patent the vaccine for personal profit.

Hospitals used the latest in technology in the operating rooms. All areas were brightly lit with no shadows.

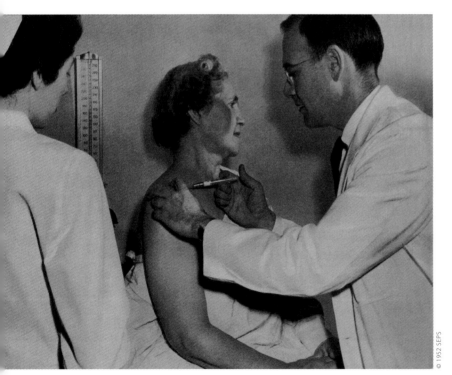

Dr. Joseph Hollander developed a new arthritis treatment and administers a shot of Compound F.

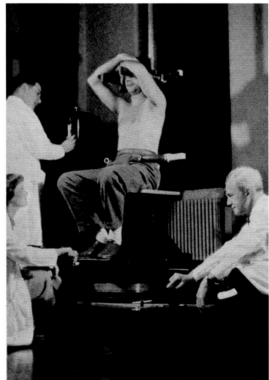

Rays from this rotating X-ray machine bombarded the patient without exposing any one area too long.

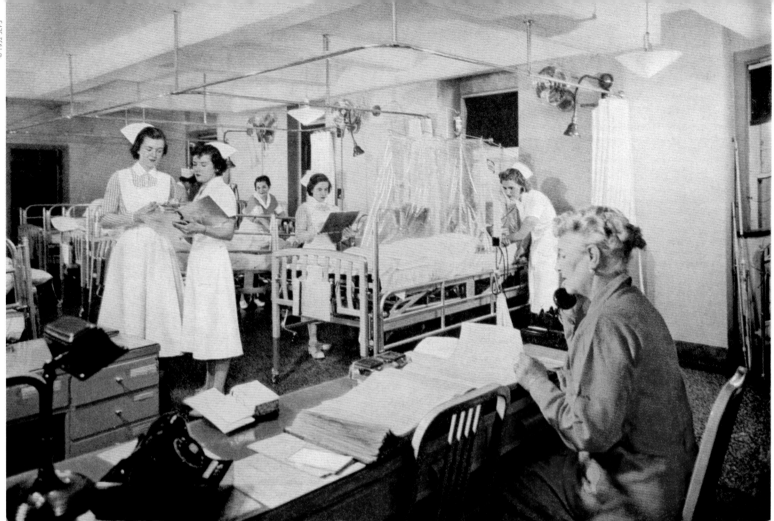

There was a renewal of hospitals with construction or renovation of facilities across the country. Hospital stays were much shorter than in the 1940s. Childbirth, which had hospitalized women for up to two weeks, now required only an average four-day stay.

Polio patients rely on the iron lung machine for breathing. Though the polio vaccine was developed in 1952, much testing was required before it was released for public use.

What Made Us Laugh

"Spread the blackberry jam thick. He won't get much of that in the French Foreign Legion."

"Will the delegation from Idaho kindly register their protests a bit more formally?"

"I thought it seemed strange that, no matter where I turned, that tree was always in front of me."

"Remember last year?...We drove all the way out here and discovered you'd forgotten the picnic lunch."

"Take a letter to the Ajax
Medical Laboratories!"

"Goodbye, Alfred. We'll see
you again in six months."

"Only 38 candles? This is a surprise party!"

"It's times like this when you
can use that extra power!"

Chevrolet matched America's highest-priced cars with this beautiful new Chevrolet Styleline. It was the lowest-priced line in its field at about $1,500.

The Hudson Hornet brought the surest, safest motoring known. With a sensational new engine, it packed real punch into the driving experience.

The Willys Station Wagon was all-steel and the rear seats could be removed to carry cargo.

The smart, new Dodge Coronet Sierra won admirers with its looks and dependable performance, selling for about $2,100.

Cars on the Highway

The automobiles that would transform the American landscape were becoming widely available in 1952 at an average car cost of $1,700. American families were buying cars with the same enthusiasm they brought to the purchase of their suburban houses. The U.S. auto industry was dominated by Detroit's Big Three: General Motors, Ford Motor Company and Chrysler Corporation. The new bywords were competition and innovation. Millions of dollars were spent to develop bigger, more powerful V-8 engines, new body styles, tailfins and lavishly chromed bumpers. Cars were closely linked with status. Virtually everybody in the middle class could afford a car. The model didn't matter as long as it was new and it was yours.

REPRINTED WITH PERMISSION OF STUDEBAKER NATIONAL MUSEUM

The excitingly styled Studebaker saved gasoline every mile.

COURTESY OF CHRYSLER GROUP LLC

The Chrysler Imperial was advertised as the new world leader in luxury cars.

This Nash had seats that reclined and could be made into beds and cost from $2,520 to $2,830.

COURTESY OF CHRYSLER GROUP LLC

COURTESY OF CHRYSLER GROUP LLC

The 1952 Kaiser claimed to have the safest front seat.

This Pontiac featured dual-range performance with spectacular power and economy.

Cadillac climaxed 50 years of progress with this Golden Anniversary edition that sold for over $7,000.

Cars on the Highway

Cruising in convertibles

U.S. automakers manufactured a broad range of convertibles. The roof was affixed to the body of the vehicle and was usually not detachable. Instead, the roof hinged and folded away and was constructed of soft or rigid material. Living was easier, less formal and more fun in a convertible. The view and the fresh air all contributed to a sense of freedom for adventurous drivers. Boys vaulted into the driver's seat instead of using the door. Girls enjoyed the feel of the wind in their hair, but complained about having their hairdos rearranged by the wind.

No car had a more perfect line and grace than a 1952 Ford Sunliner.

The Oldsmobile Ninety-Eight brought back the ultra-long look in convertibles and sold for about $2,500.

Lincoln put modern living on wheels.

Thrifty, power-packed and luxurious—the Packard had it all.

Mercury advertised an advanced V-8 engine that had greater horsepower with high-compression performance.

DeSoto's Fire Dome 8 premiered full-power steering, power braking and America's finest no-shift driving.

Corn was picked, left on the cob and dried in corn cribs.

The Allis-Chalmers two-row cotton picker could pick up to 50 times as fast as a man by hand.

Many small farms kept a variety of critters ranging from pigs, cattle and sheep to chickens. Children in the family were often in charge of feeding.

Working Country Style

Day-to-day life in rural America was quiet and pastoral. Family members young and old labored side by side and valued a good work ethic. Yet, the number of family farms began to dwindle, while the average farm size increased. The chances were high that farm children would not follow in their parents' footsteps and take over the operation as many were lured to higher-paying jobs in the cities. At this time, great strides were made in the area of agricultural research, and farmers in the United States adopted new crops and livestock technologies. As a result, millions of people worldwide were saved from starvation.

Ranchers rounded up wild mustangs, brought them down from the high meadows and broke them for riding.

Silage was fodder, which was harvested while green and stored in a silo to feed cattle and sheep.

City Life

American urban society was nearing its peak. Downtown was in its prime and it united cities, whose neighborhoods were each a city within a city. Many families had lived in their neighborhoods for decades and had relatives a few blocks away. Housewives and children filled stoops and porches during the day and walked to nearby grocery stores, movie houses, tea rooms, boutiques, barbershops and five and dime stores. Many of the people living in the new suburbs relied on these city businesses and worked in the factories and office buildings. In the evenings, long, sleek cars filled with well-dressed people cruised to movies, theaters, dances and restaurants.

THE GOODYEAR TIRE & RUBBER COMPANY

Downtown New York was the heart of the city, where neon lights blinked to advertise the stores and entertainment found there.

© 1952 SEPS

Cities offered numerous restaurants with wide varieties of food served.

San Francisco men patronize a sidewalk-stand flower vender.

For the sophisticated, going out in the evening called for a jacket and tie for men, and gloves and high heels for women.

"Dave, I'll meet you in the outer lobby after the show."

For those who did not know how to dance, neighborhood dance studios offered lessons on the latest trends.

This building housed Curtis Publishing offices and printing operations.

The Saturday Evening Post magazine was printed by Curtis Publishing in Philadelphia.

Rocky Marciano acknowledges cheers as he is crowned the new heavyweight boxing champion at Municipal Stadium in Philadelphia.

American Bandstand had its start in Philadelphia.

City Life

Philadelphia

Philadelphia is the centerpiece of early American history. Patriotism and love of country are stimulated at shrines of American freedom, such as Independence Hall. The Continental Congress met there and the Declaration of Independence and Constitution had their roots in the building. Filmed in Philadelphia, *The Greatest Show on Earth*, a movie following the dramatic lives of circus employees, won the Academy Award for Best Picture. Rocky Marciano won his heavyweight boxing championship in Philadelphia. He is the only boxing champion to ever retire undefeated. Philadelphia is known for its food, specifically soft pretzels, hoagies and cheesesteak sandwiches.

A group of attentive visitors hear the story of the famous Liberty Bell.

A view of bustling Market Street in Philadelphia.

Tribute to Artist John Falter

John Falter was a Nebraska-born illustrator born in 1910. He showed an interest in art from a very early age, and by high school was refining this interest into painted murals. He studied art at the Kansas City Art Institute. Although jobs were scarce during the Great Depression, John managed to find employment illustrating for magazines and later acquired advertising clients such as Gulf Oil, Four Roses Whisky and Arrow Shirts. Falter's first cover for *The Saturday Evening Post* was a portrait of the magazine's founder, Benjamin Franklin, in 1943. He eventually painted 129 *Post* covers, most of them reflections from his own life.

John Falter's father told him he would not be an artist until he painted a cover for *The Saturday Evening Post*. Family, friends and hometown America were his usual subjects.

The portrait of Benjamin Franklin, left, was Falter's first cover for *The Saturday Evening Post*.

During the hottest days of summer, children headed to ponds and swimming pools to cool off and splash in the water.

Families loaded the wicker picnic basket and heavy tin cooler into the family sedan and drove to the nearest park.

FAMOUS BIRTHDAYS
Dan Aykroyd, July 1 Canadian actor and comedian
John Tesh, July 9 composer, musician and radio host

Children looked forward to summer camps, where many pillow fights took place after camp counselors called for lights out.

Summer Fun

It's summertime, and the living is easy. Families went on vacation, saw ball games and visited the beach. Picnics were a fun alternative to eating at restaurants. Children rode their bikes, circling the block and visiting friends. Boys hung baseball gloves from the handlebars as they pedaled to the local sandlot. Summer camps offered a range of activities: survival skills, nature study, sports and arts and crafts. Evening campfires were the setting for songs, storytelling and marshmallow roasting.

Beaches were popular summer destinations; many with amusement-park rides and boardwalks along the shoreline.

Summer camps offered a variety of activities, like this monkey bridge.

Hours were spent fishing and inspired stories about the fish that got away.

America Travels

In 1952, most American tourists traveled to locations within the continental United States. Many chose to journey to one or more of the many national parks and monuments scattered across the country. They explored Florida and the Gulf Coast, California and the Southwest. Railroads still transported over 75 percent of distant passenger traffic. The wealthy and elite opted to travel by luxury trains that reflected the latest in style, design and technological improvements. Streamlined sleeper cars, dining cars and lounge cars were pulled by diesel locomotives. Bus travel was less expensive. Greyhound advertised complete pleasure trips, including hotels, transportation and sightseeing. A four-day trip to Washington, D.C. cost just $23. Five days touring Colorado Springs was advertised for about $38. Of course, fare from your hometown was extra. A vacation to great cities, northern lakes, scenic California and sunny Florida was affordable for many when traveling by bus.

Receiving a royal send-off at the train station.

Pennsylvania Railroad offered air-conditioning, colorful decor, fluorescent lighting, panoramic windows, enclosed telephone rooms and handsomely furnished lounge cars to make travel a pleasant experience.

Greyhound advertized comfortable travel by bus with friendly, interesting people. Agents arranged trips south during the winter.

Train parlor cars were as comfortable as the living room at home.

Fine dining was available on a Union Pacific train.

Air travel was an adventure and this boy is prepared, though he looks more like an astronaut than a typical airline passenger.

The berths on Pan American's double-decked clippers were larger than those on trains.

Americans could travel in style aboard Pan American's giant double-decked airliners. The lower-deck lounge gave passengers a chance to stroll and enjoy refreshments in flight. Even a seven-course champagne dinner was included.

America Travels

By air

Prosperity meant that Americans strove to enlarge their travel horizons. The number of Americans traveling abroad increased greatly when travel became available by air. Round-trip fare to Nice, France was advertised for $517 and Hawaii was accessible for $240. The commercial airlines competed fiercely with each other to offer faster flights to farther destinations. As airplanes accommodated more passengers, the airlines began offering different grades of seating. First class provided a larger seat and more amenities, but coach offered a lower rate.

TWA advertised genuinely friendly hostesses who anticipated needs, catered to every wish and satisfied appetites with delicious meals.

Successful businessmen traveled by plane to key cities coast to coast.

"Relax, mister, we'll let you know as soon as it shows up!"

Summer Olympics

Helsinki, Finland

The 1952 Summer Olympic Games started in spectacular fashion when runner Paavo Nurmi, at age 55, entered with the Olympic flame and lit the cauldron. The most impressive achievement of the games was by long-distance runner, Emil Zatopek of Czechoslovakia, who became the only person in Olympic history to win the 5,000-meter, 10,000-meter and marathon runs at the same Olympics. The Soviet Union entered the games for the first time. Although their athletes were housed separately, warnings that Cold War rivalries would lead to clashes proved unfounded. The Soviet women gymnasts won the team competition. Dr. Samuel Lee was the first Asian-American to win an Olympic gold medal for the United States in platform diving. The United States won the medal count with 76 medals and the Soviets were second with 71.

The official poster for the 1952 Helsinki, Finland summer Olympics.

American athlete Robert Mathias grimaces with the effort of his leap. He was the first Olympian to successfully defend his decathlon title.

Finnish runner Paavo Nurmi, a former gold medalist, lights the Olympic flame at the opening ceremonies.

Prince Axel of Denmark presents a gold medal to Malvin Whitfield of the United States, winner of the 800-meter final.

The Metro Daily News

FINAL EDITION

JULY 21, 1952

7.8 EARTHQUAKE (RICHTER SCALE) SHAKES KERN COUNTY, CALIF. AND KILLS 14

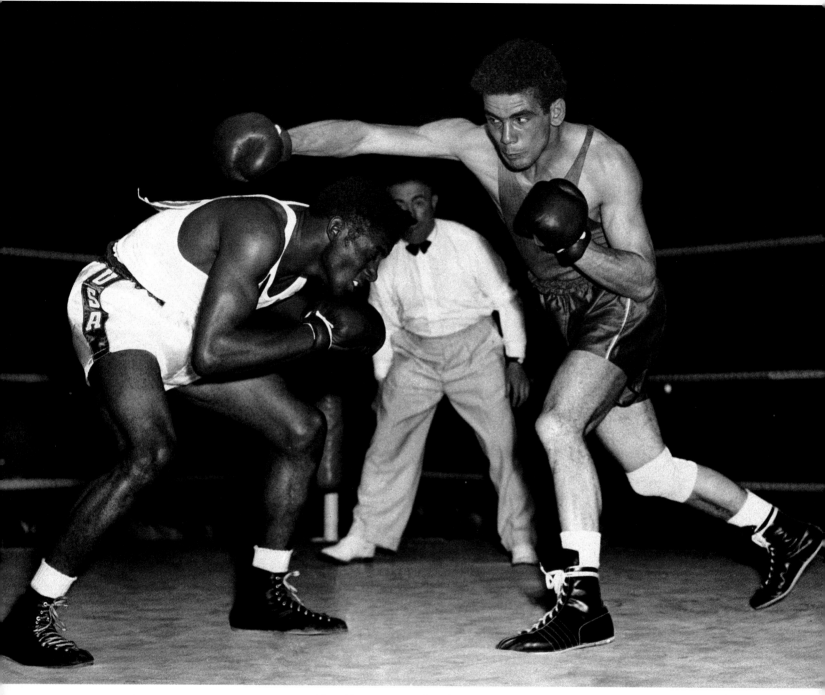

Floyd Patterson, left, of New York City ducks under a right hook from Omar Tebbaka of France. Patterson won the middleweight Olympic boxing match on points.

Summer Olympics

Athletes in action

A total of 4,955 athletes from 69 countries participated in the 1952 summer Olympics. Each athlete had their own personal story of struggles and victories. American Floyd Patterson delivered a number of punches on the way to his boxing Olympic gold medal, but it may have been his fights outside the ring that made him great. He overcame poverty and prejudice to excel at his sport. Asian-American diver Sammy Lee also overcame discrimination before attaining his goals to be a diver and a medical physician.

Sammy Lee, of the United States, won a gold medal for men's high diving.

Members of the U.S. Women's 400-meter relay team cavort on the field after winning the event and setting a world record. Left to right: Catherine Hardy, Barbara Jones, Mae Faggs and Janet Moreau.

The United States played the Soviet Union in the men's basketball gold medal game with the Americans winning.

World Events

Many Americans were awakened to the Holocaust in 1952 with the English-language publication of *The Diary of Anne Frank*. King George VI of England died on Feb. 6. His daughter Elizabeth, who was away on a trip, flew back as Queen Elizabeth II. For years, Fulgencio Batista ruled Cuba from behind the scenes. On March 10, 1952, he achieved absolute power in a coup. In December of 1952, a fog descended upon London. Because of air pollution from burning coal and diesel buses trapped by a heavy layer of cold air, 4,000 people died from respiratory problems. Another 8,000 died in the months that followed.

The Diary of Anne Frank has been translated into many languages and more than 25 million copies have been sold. Anne brought to life her own experiences of hiding from the Nazis during World War II.

New Cuban leader Fulgencio Batista smiles with upraised hands as he is surrounded by Cuban soldiers during the revolution in 1952.

A great smog befell London. The smog was a horrific disaster that killed thousands and was an important event that led to the modern environmental movement.

England mourns as the coffin of Britain's King George VI nears St. George's Chapel in Windsor Castle on Feb. 14, 1952.

© THE ASSOCIATED PRESS

The chain of command during battle.

Korean War medical corpsmen assist in helping wounded infantrymen following a battle.

The striking power of a big Navy carrier consisted of approximately 100 highly versatile airplanes.

Unrest in Korea

When World War II ended in 1945, Korea, which had been occupied by the Japanese, was divided by an agreement between the United States and the Soviet Union. When the Soviet-supported North Korean Army invaded the South in 1950, the Cold War reached a boiling point and the United Nations authorized forces to push them back. In 1952, the army began a campaign of psychological warfare, broadcasting in Korean to Communist troops urging surrender. In May, the United States dropped bombs and gallons of napalm on the ancient city of Suan. In July, communist troop headquarters was found at Pyongyan, North Korea, and in August, troops hammered the headquarters with the largest single-day air raid of the war.

An F2H twin-jet Banshee returns from combat over North Korea.

Battle-equipped Marines land at the front lines.

The Metro Daily News

FINAL EDITION

AUGUST 6, 1952

SATCHEL PAIGE, 47, BECOMES THE OLDEST PITCHER TO WIN A COMPLETE SHUTOUT

That's Entertainment

Listening to the radio

Even though television use was on the upswing, not many American households owned one. Most American households had at least one radio, and everyone thought it was a well-entrenched media. When listenership started to plummet, radio networks fought television's inroads by hiring more stars in longer variety shows. *Whispering Streets*, a romantic soap-opera drama, debuted, but *Mr. District Attorney* and *The Green Hornet* ended their runs. *Amos 'n' Andy*, one of the most popular shows in 20th century entertainment, continued to be the No. 1 radio show. *Duffy's Tavern*, ranked third, was hailed from the start by critics and whole neighborhoods of working-class listeners alike, a duo that didn't often see eye to eye.

Amos 'n' Andy, staring comedians Charles Corell and Freeman Gosden, was the top-ranked show of the year. Radios became more compact and portable. Zenith sold the two models at right for $25 and $124.

Duffy's Tavern studio members are taping an episode of their radio show.

Fibber McGee and Molly was one of the cornerstones of the radio experience. The comedy was about a typical couple in a typical town. Most of the show's humor relied on recurring gags, unseen regulars and punch lines that popped up here and there for years.

Radio Stars & Hits of 1952

Amos 'n' Andy

Bing Crosby

Duffy's Tavern

Edgar Bergen and Charlie McCarthy

Escape

Falcon

Fibber McGee and Molly

The Green Hornet

Gunsmoke

Mr. Keen, Tracer of Lost Persons

Mysterious Traveler

Shadow

Sherlock Holmes

Smilin' Ed's Buster Brown Gang

Suspense

This Is Your FBI

Whistler

Yours Truly, Johnny Dollar

Top Hits of 1952

"Wheel of Fortune"
Kay Starr

"Auf Wiederseh'n Sweetheart"
Vera Lynn

"Blue Tango"
Leroy Anderson

"You Belong to Me"
Jo Stafford

"I Went to Your Wedding"
Patti Page

"Why Don't You Believe Me"
Joni James

"Here in My Heart"
Al Martino

"I Saw Mommy Kissing Santa Claus"
Jimmy Boyd

"Delicado"
Percy Faith & His Orchestra

"It's In the Book"
Johnny Standley

Kay Starr began singing at the age of nine. Each day when she returned home from school, she would give concerts to the chickens as they sat in their roosts. It wasn't long until her talent was discovered.

© GETTY IMAGES

That's Entertainment

Enjoying the music

Many of the big bands of the 1940s had disappeared, opening the door for individual vocalists. Kay Starr, whose deep husky voice was her trademark, sang "Wheel of Fortune", which became the top 1952 hit. Singer Al Martino combined charisma and a unique vocal style for success. "Here in My Heart" was his debut and the ballad immediately sold over one million copies. Vera Lynn, with her sweet voice and girl-next-door persona, was known during World War II as the Forces' Sweetheart. Her popularity easily survived the wartime years. Her most successful recording was ironically "Auf Wiederseh'n Sweetheart", a song with a German theme.

Popular British singer Vera Lynn sings for the British Broadcasting Co.

Crooner Al Martino poses for a portrait.

Zenith's new Malabar table radio-phonograph featured "big set" tone quality for $100.

That's Entertainment

Going to the movies

Movies in 1952 were an entertainment bargain at 60 cents, but weekly movie attendance began dropping. In response, Hollywood began experimenting with technical gimmicks that might lure people back into theaters. Many larger-budget films already were in color and had high-fidelity sound, so 3-D movies were introduced, a short-lived fad. Many film critics and fans consider *Singin' in the Rain* America's greatest movie musical. Dancer-actor Gene Kelly was at his creative peak. Kelly's performance of the title number remains one of cinema's best-loved sequences. *The Bad and the Beautiful* was an entertaining melodrama that told the story of the ruthless rise and fall of a tyrannical, manipulative Hollywood movie tycoon. The film earned five Academy Awards.

This formally attired audience sports the latest in moviegoing accessories at the premiere of the African adventure *Bwana Devil*, the first 3-D movie.

Gene Kelly co-directed *Singin' in the Rain*, drawing career-making performances from Donald O'Connor, Jean Hagen and newcomer Debbie Reynolds. Donald O'Connor won a Golden Globe award for Best Actor for his efforts.

SINGIN' IN THE RAIN

Starring:
GENE KELLY
DONALD O'CONNOR
DEBBIE REYNOLDS

M-G-M's TECHNICOLOR Musical Treasure!

JEAN HAGEN · MILLARD MITCHELL and CYD CHARIS
Story and Screen Play by BETTY COMDEN and ADOLPH GREEN · Suggested by the Song "SINGIN' IN THE RAIN" · Lyrics by ARTHUR FRE
Music by NACIO HERB BROWN · Directed by GENE KELLY · STANLEY DONEN · Produced by ARTHUR FREED

Tops at the Box Office

The Greatest Show on Earth
The Bad and the Beautiful
The Snows of Kilimanjaro
Ivanhoe
Singin' in the Rain
Sailor Beware
Moulin Rouge
Hans Christian Andersen
Affair in Trinidad
Monkey Business

Charlton Heston and Betty Hutton star as circus artists in the film *The Greatest Show On Earth*, directed by Cecil B. DeMille for Paramount. This movie won an Academy Award for Best Picture.

American actors Dick Powell and Gloria Grahame in a still from the film *The Bad and the Beautiful*, directed by Vincente Minnelli. Gloria received the Academy Award for Best Supporting Actress in this movie.

FAMOUS BIRTHDAYS

Debbie Meyer, August 14
Olympic swimmer
Patrick Swayze, August 18 actor and dancer

Croquet was a well-liked summer game for everyone. All that was needed was a lawn and a set of mallots, balls and hoops.

Comic books were full of good fun, clean enjoyment and happy adventures.

Television took center stage, even in the midst of a birthday party.

The Metro Daily News

FINAL EDITION

THE WEATHER
City and Snow—Rain, Snow, Colder

VOLUME 67 — No. 161

SEPTEMBER 8, 1952

ERNEST HEMMINGWAY'S
THE OLD MAN AND THE SEA
IS PUBLISHED

Leisurely Pastimes

Many Americans floated through the year on a cloud of prosperity and family values. The economy was good, and there was extra money for hobbies and activities. Modern home conveniences allowed for more free time for leisurely family activities such as croquet, a favorite lawn game. Children were not as involved in outside activities beyond Little League Baseball and an occasional Scout meeting, and that meant more family time. Comic books were favorite reading material for children, ranging from Donald Duck to Little Lulu and from Bugs Bunny to Tarzan. Television continued its upward spiral. Families often centered their evenings and weekends around their big boxes with little screens. Summers were filled with golfing, fishing and hiking.

Men and women practice their golf swings at the driving range.

Watching salmon swim upstream was nearly as exciting as fishing for them.

Hiking and picnicking were often combined to fill a leisurely family afternoon.

Families marked yearly birthdays with the traditional cake and candles.

Family Life

Families were larger with the postwar flood of newborns, but in general the small size of most homes was not a problem. Kids didn't mind sharing bedrooms and the only real hardship was having just one bathroom. Mom got the day off to a good start with a full breakfast and dad was greeted with open arms when he returned home from work. Church was an important part of life for many families. Most churches were smaller with no more than a few hundred members, and people were close to each other. Family time was valued and there was time to sit and read together. Birthdays were the highlight celebrations of the year.

Dad's arrival home was an anticipated daily event.

Clothes were passed on to siblings though a few alterations were typically needed.

Attending church was also a social event, with members greeting each other and catching up on news.

Occasionally, a father would care for the children while the mother would take a much-deserved break from her routine to go shopping.

Mothers and fathers took time to read to their children.

Soda fountains offered soft drinks and various concoctions made with ice cream and were popular after-school gathering places for adolescents.

HIRES TO YOU!

Hires Root Beer was made from roots, barks and berries.

7UP was the all-family drink. Advertisements read "'Fresh up' with Seven-Up!"

Beverages the Whole Family Loved

Numerous thirst-quenching beverages were available in 1952. Coca-Cola was part of a fun, carefree American lifestyle. The imagery of its advertising—happy couples at the drive-in, carefree moms driving big yellow convertibles—reflected the spirit of the times. Nestlé Quik provided kids and families with fun ways to turn milk into an irresistibly delicious drink. Ovaltine was also added to milk. Based on malt extract, eggs and cocoa, it was advertised for its ability to build body, brain and nerves to the highest efficiency. With the overall increase in the standard of living came the "cocktail culture," a way for men and women to unwind from the workday. Cocktails were usually a blend of gin and tonic.

When on the go, a stop at the familiar red Coca-Cola vending machine was like meeting up with an old friend.

Everybody loves NEHI ORANGE

Nehi was a fruit-flavored soda that became well-liked.

Coffee was still the most frequently consumed drink as a breakfast wake-up or with desserts after dinner.

Kids Being Kids

Life was not as complicated for children. There was less structured time, which allowed for more imaginative play along with the inevitable episodes of mischief. Summer, with no schoolwork to think about, was prime time for kids to get into trouble. Children rarely think about potential consequences. The deed simply sounds like great fun at the time. Remembering your own childhood naughtiness? Everyone has a favorite story to pass on. We laugh at the antics, but rarely recall the punishment doled out by parents who more often than not hid smiles while they disciplined.

This boy was sent to bed during an adult party, but decided to investigate the contents of the ladies' purses instead.

Inspired by television westerns, playing cowboys and Indians filled many hours.

Getting dirty was so much fun. Mud was a readily available ingredient for making mud pies, but playing in the muck and mire meant extra laundry for Mom.

FAMOUS BIRTHDAYS
Jimmy Connors, September 2
tennis player
Christopher Reeve, September 25
actor and activist

NO GIRLS ALLOWED

"He's up!"

Tree houses were favorite private retreats for boys. No girls were allowed, but the dog was an honored guest.

Kids Being Kids

From morning to night

Norman Rockwell

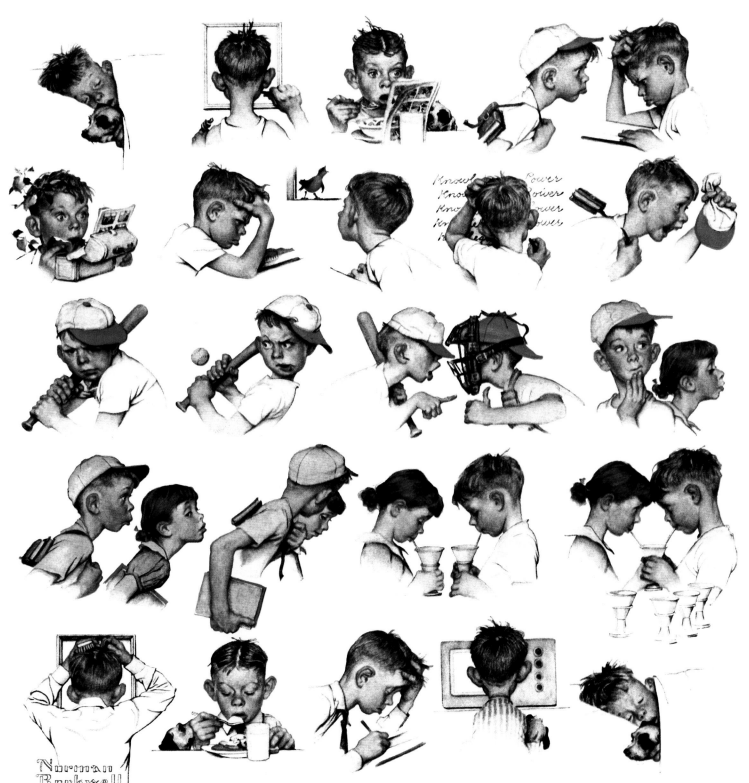

A Mom's Busy Day

Once the babies were born, mothers were expected to stay home to raise the children. Disposable diapers were not yet available, which meant using cloth diapers that required laundering. Automatic washers were common but clothes dryers were not, so most families used a marvelous device known as a clothesline. Many items needed to be ironed. Food was prepared from scratch, a time-consuming process, and meals were real sit-down family affairs. After each meal, there were stacks of dishes to wash by hand. Along with caring for sick children, chauffeuring for events and grocery shopping, mothers earned their rest each night.

Under Mom's supervision, daughters were taught to bake from scratch.

Mom mediates a sibling argument.

Mom served homemade food.

Moms acted as 24-hour, on-call nurses.

Grocery shopping for a large family was a sizeable task, so moms were grateful for help putting away the purchases.

Laundry consumed a great deal of a woman's day.

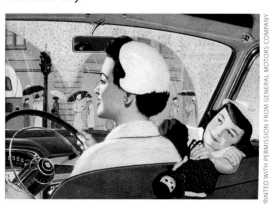

Many families only had one car so Mom found herself being the chauffeur for everyone.

Women ironed nearly everything.

The band director needed nerves of steel to survive all the screeching sounds produced by beginner musicians.

One of the rewards of being a well-behaved child was being named safety patrolman.

Graduation was a major life event that represented the end of childhood.

New, single school buildings replaced many small country schools.

School-Day Memories

Parents were determined their children would receive a quality education and be prepared to land a good job. There were few kindergartens or preschools, so kids started first grade at age 6. Most teachers and principals used paddles applied to the backsides of unruly children to maintain discipline. Few new schools were built during the 1940s, but post-war prosperity and a booming population resulted in new, modern buildings that were airy, clean and sunlit. After-school activities added excitement. Baseball was the most popular sport and schools had boys baseball and basketball teams while girls also had their cheerleading squads. Other school activities included plays, dances and band concerts.

Cheerleaders celebrated when the home team won, but a fierce losing effort was mourned by all.

Recess wasn't the only time children exercised. Many walked to school, though children in the country were transported by the big yellow school bus.

Champions in Sports

Sam Snead won the Masters Tournament at Augusta, Georgia.

Modern conveniences allowed people of all ages to spend longer periods of time enjoying sports. Television now brought all types of sporting events into family homes. At first, it was feared TV would reduce attendance at the events. Just the opposite proved to be true. Fans became more attracted to favorite teams and athletic heroes, so they paid record amounts of money to watch them play in person. Wins were celebrated by large, cheering crowds of fans. People thronged to witness golfer Sam Snead's win at the Masters Tournament. He wowed golf enthusiasts with his long drives that earned him the nickname "Slammin' Sam."

The 1952 Minneapolis Lakers were the world champions of basketball.

The Metro Daily News

OCTOBER 7

BOB HORN'S BANDSTAND DEBUTS ON PHILADELPHIA'S TV STATION WFIL-TV

This show later becomes *American Bandstand* and Dick Clark joins as host in 1955.

Well-known golfer Betsy Rawls won six tournaments in 1952 and was the LPGA Tour money leader at $14,505.

The Detroit Red Wings did not lose a single game in their Stanley Cup triumph over the Montreal Canadians.

Troy Ruttman won the 36th Indianapolis 500 race with a record-breaking speed of 128.922 mph.

Boxer Joey Maxim, 2nd from right, defeated Sugar Ray Robinson for the light heavyweight championship at Yankee Stadium.

Maureen Connolly receives the silver salver trophy from the Duchess of Kent after winning the women's singles tennis championship at Wimbledon.

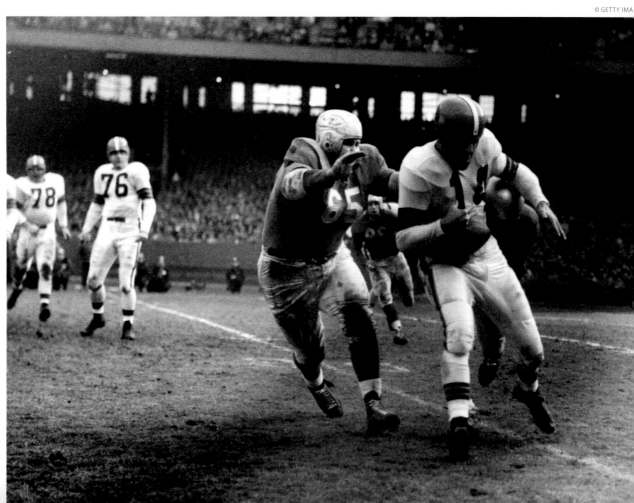

Cleveland Browns Hall of Fame quarterback Otto Graham tries to avoid being tackled in the loss to the Detroit Lions for the NFL championship game at Cleveland Municipal Stadium in Cleveland, Ohio.

Champions in Sports

Proud athletes

A new group of memorable champions was crowned in 1952. Born Giuseppe Antonio Berardinelli, boxer Joey Maxim took his ring name from the Maxim machine gun, based on his ability to throw rapid numbers of punches. His talent earned him a championship. Maureen Connolly, Wimbledon tennis tournament champion, was known for her rigorous practice regimen. The Cleveland Browns defeated the Detroit Lions 17-7 on Dec. 28 to become the NFL champs. The American Girls' Baseball League was started during World War II, to keep the sport alive while most men were serving in the war, and continued to be popular in 1952. The girls practiced and played hard, but were expected to maintain lady-like behavior at all times.

Left-handed hurler Bob Kuzava is flanked by Mickey Mantle, left, and Gene Woodling in the New York Yankees locker room after winning the seventh and final game of the 1952 World Series.

Betty Foss of the Fort Wayne Daisies was the MVP of the American Girls' Baseball League.

The South Bend Blue Sox team receives the trophy as American Girls' Baseball League champions.

What Made Us Laugh

"This is something I hadn't figured on."

"Not me! I opened the door last time!"

"We'd better check up on this guy! That little dream house he's describing sounds like <u>this</u> house!"

"Oops! Missed it again."

"No, I don't want to retain my individuality.
I want to look like Ava Gardner."

"Another crack like that and I'll pull your
beautiful blond hair out by its ugly dark roots!"

"Guess what we're having for
supper tonight … and where."

"Substitution—Malkowski for O'Brien."

Leading Ladies of *The Post*

Take a peek at some of the art inside the covers of *The Saturday Evening Post*. The Leading Ladies of *The Post* are a collection of images from regularly-featured, steamy romance stories. Illustrators were challenged to interpret these stories on canvas and we have included a sampling of the Leading Ladies of 1952. The sultry fashion-forward heroines of the tales are featured along with the original article captions.

What did the artist see? An innocent childlike girl. What did everyone else see? That dangerous woman known as "The Desert Orchid."

He knew she loved him. He couldn't believe that she would brush him aside, that she was so determined to become a hired bride.

She said she wanted to marry him, but he knew better. She was a spoiled kid, and this was just another rich girl's whim.

FAMOUS BIRTHDAYS

Dave Collins, October 20
professional baseball player
Annie Potts, October 28 actress

He had kissed her once and tried to forget her ever since. His work kept him far too busy for marriage.

Carried away by her beauty, the young man forgot the one thing he should have remembered: This woman could ruin him.

She was darned if she'd go on helping her fiancé entertain another girl. No man of hers could play around with two girls at once.

Women were ready for the Easter Parade dressed in suits, gloves and hats.

Little girls imagined being grown-up and glamorous.

Short scarves added pizzazz to any outfit.

Fashion Trends

Women's fashions reflected the primness that society expected. Waists were tight and often pinched to the point of agony by girdles. Skirts were A-line or full and hemlines reached well below the knee. Little girls also wore dresses and circle skirts were made with enough fabric to make a 360-degree circle, perfect for swirling and twirling. New Orlon acrylic fabric was introduced. Sweaters stayed soft and held shape and size after washing. You could kiss your sweater stretcher goodbye. Skirts shunned wrinkles and the pleats stayed put.

Every girl's favorite school outfit was a soft fitted sweater paired with a full, pleated skirt.

Most women wanted to look glamorous. A variety of girdles existed to help achieve those contours.

Women wore stretchy nylons with seams in the back. It was important to keep the seams straight, which required frequent checking.

Fashion Trends

Men looking their best

American businessmen dressed in dark suits that featured crisp, perfect tailoring. Though the suits were understated, socks and ties were not. Colors and patterns were all the rage, from plaid socks to hand-painted ties. Shoes needed to be fashionable, but comfort was still top priority. The required hat was "mirror-styled" to look right from every angle. During leisure hours, men dressed in slightly looser, more colorful clothing. Wash and wear cotton flannel shirts in bright plaids were perfect choices for relaxation time. Work clothes were made of heavy denim for long wear.

Men's socks were often patterned and there were many styles to choose from.

1952 HART SCHAFFNER & MARX

1952 INTERWOVEN

Tweed fabrics used to be strictly for the great outdoors. In 1952 they were equally smart and appropriate for business wear.

The Metro Daily News

FINAL EDITION

THE WEATHER
City still Rain—Rain.
Snow, Colder

VOLUME 97 — No. 781

FIVE CENTS

NOVEMBER 4, 1952

DWIGHT D. EISENHOWER ELECTED PRESIDENT OF THE UNITED STATES

Richard M. Nixon is Eisenhower's Vice President.

Handsome, durable-grain leather shoes could be purchased for $10 to $17.

"… Notice how a striped suit makes you appear taller …"

Jerry Marcus

Smartly tailored, 100 percent wool suits were considered an excellent buy at $50.

Dress shirts were fitted with "non-wilt" collars.

This Fifth Avenue Knox hat sold for $10.

While Art Linkletter chews his fingers, his dutiful family chortles at his weekly television program, *Life With Linkletter*.

The Linkletters peek into the Caroline Leonetti Charm School in Hollywood. The comic was a part owner of the place.

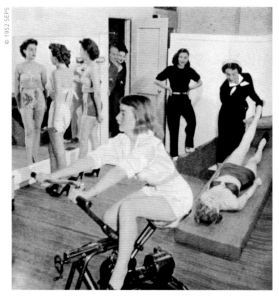

Art, in the red chair, has a script conference at the office of Guedel Productions.

Linkletter plays with his kids at their home in Holmby Hills, Calif. Although his programs were described as low comedy, his weekly audience was about 20 million.

Funny Man, Art Linkletter

Art Linkletter was a master of the gentle art of getting people to make fools of themselves in public. He made a fortune out of slapstick with his radio and TV shows, *People Are Funny, House Party* and *Life With Linkletter*. The audience-participation shows proved to be a success among viewers. Linkletter was a benevolent clown who never had a serious thought, yet he was educated to be a teacher of English. He was particularly skilled at interviewing children, whose candid remarks were his shows most precious moments. He lived a full and fruitful life entertaining both young and old and died at age 97.

The Los Angeles Board of Education provides Linkletter with a group of young children. Here, Art tries his charm on the kids.

Betty Hutton, a guest star, kisses a sailor during a warm-up of *House Party*, one of Linkletter's three programs.

Democratic candidate Adlai Stevenson tips his hat upon his arrival at the Democratic National Convention in Chicago, Ill. He initially declined the offer to run for president, believing Eisenhower was unbeatable, but later reconsidered.

"Don't keep insisting they look at your record—they might!"

Presidential Election

The campaign trail

President Truman chose not to run for another term in 1952 and the Democratic nomination went to Illinois Governor Adlai Stevenson. The Republican candidate, Dwight D. Eisenhower, was one of the most respected figures in the United States. Ike, as he was nicknamed, commanded the Allied forces in Europe during World War II. The Republicans played on Eisenhower's popularity with the campaign slogan, "I Like Ike." They concentrated on the themes of "Korea, Communism and Corruption." In return, the Democrats accused Eisenhower's running-mate Richard M. Nixon of accepting gifts in return for political favors. Nixon defended himself on national television, showing the growing importance of television in politics.

President Harry Truman meets with Governor Adlai Stephenson of Illinois and Senator John Sparkman of Alabama in the oval office. Stevenson had just accepted the Democratic nomination for President.

Clark Gable and Jinx Falkenberg were among the entertainers at the Ike rally.

© 1952 SEPS

Ticket for admission to a campaign rally to see Dwight D. Eisenhower.

CLEVELAND PUBLIC AUDITORIUM
East 6th at Lakeside — Cleveland, Ohio

PRESIDENTIAL RALLY

SEPT. 23 1952 — *Dwight D. Eisenhower*

TUESDAY EVENING
Sept. 23, 1952
Doors Open at 6:30 P.M.

ADMIT ONE
RESERVED SECTION
UNTIL 7:30 P.M. ONLY
Present Ticket At Door

DWIGHT D. EISENHOWER
PRESIDENTIAL LIBRARY
& MUSEUM

Richard M. Nixon and Dwight D. Eisenhower raise their hands in victory at the GOP convention, the first to be broadcast on television.

THEY'RE FOR YOU
IKE DICK

The Republican slogan "I Like Ike" was seen everywhere.

LET'S BACK IKE

I LIKE IKE

Norman Rockwell painted the above portrait and said, "We had to work hard and fast. But Dwight Eisenhower has a way of keeping you calm while a job gets done."

Artist Rockwell said, "What a mobile face he has. He registered grave contemplation when told he should be an artists' model, then cracked it up into a grin."

Vice President-elect Richard M. Nixon with his wife, Pat, and their two daughters, Julie and Patricia.

Wife Mamie seemed close at hand in Eisenhower's thinking, a present source of inspiration. He spoke of her as if she were right in his office.

Presidential Election

Dwight D. Eisenhower wins!

When Americans went to the polls in November, 1952, the result was a landslide victory for Eisenhower and the Republicans. Eisenhower won with 34 million votes as opposed to 27.3 million for Stevenson. As the American face of the Allied victory in World War II, Eisenhower was revered as a hero nationwide. With an easy grin and grandfatherly charm, he was widely viewed as an affable, decent man. Though he privately battled a furious temper, Ike and wife Mamie brought an air of decorum to Washington.

In 1952, most voters entered a curtained booth and hand-wrote their choices on a ballot.

President-elect Dwight D. Eisenhower with his family before the election. By his side are his grandson Dwight David II, his daughter-in-law Mrs. John Eisenhower, holding baby daughter Susan Elaine, his granddaughter Barbara Ann and his wife, Mamie.

Treasured Moments

In 1952, children felt more secure and could usually count on finding Mom at home at the end of the school day. She could most often be found in the kitchen, getting an early start on supper, and sometimes there would be milk and cookies ready for a snack. Most important of all, she was interested in hearing how the day went. Dads worked hard all week and probably would have preferred to do other things during their leisure time, but precious memories were created by the time spent with their offspring. Grandparents were a vital part of the family unit and helped instill values and morals.

Dad was a son's greatest hero when he took time to teach the basics of home repair.

"Did you hear that big clap of thunder last night?"

Searching for the perfect pumpkin to carve at Halloween was extra special when Grandpa was in charge of the outing.

If living close by, Grandma was an available, interested listener whether children needed advice or wanted to recall a special event of the day.

When Dad came home from work, the family was complete.

Going shopping with Mom was an exciting occasion filled with chatter and giggles.

JOHN FALTER

Christmas Traditions

The very best times were at Christmas. Santa arrived to take charge of the opening of the season. Parents would bundle up the kids, put them in the car and drive downtown to see the Christmas decorations. All the stores sparkled with lights and music, and people filled them during the last-minute, gift-buying rush. Children looked in the store windows, mesmerized by the mechanical toys, tinsel and glitter. It didn't matter if the tree was freshly cut or artificial, decorating it with baubles, bells and strands of popcorn renewed appreciation for the magic of the season. Churches featured special programs filled with music and the retelling of the Christmas story.

Shopping for the perfect gift, parties and a white-bearded replica of Santa all helped to make the season bright.

Children's choirs raised sweet, high voices to traditional tunes like "Away in a Manger" or "Silent Night."

Christmas Traditions

Surprises under the tree

Christmas day was the most anticipated event of the year. Most children had difficulty sleeping on Christmas Eve in anticipation of the biggest, most varied and most exciting collection of gifts ever. Parents were roused from their sleep before the sun peeked over the horizon as eager offspring bounced on the bed, unable to wait a single moment longer to open the presents. Mr. Potato Head was the new sought-after toy. Among the top toys for the year were Lincoln Logs, Tinker Toys, the official "Tom Corbett" Space Academy play set, Mary Hartline and Betsy McCall dolls and the Toni doll for the budding beautician. A new television usually topped the gift list for parents.

It was a merry Christmas indeed when a new television was found under the tree.

© 1952 SEP

The Metro Daily News

THE WEATHER
City of Snow-Rain.
Snow, Colder
Much in Days Before

FINAL
EDITION

20 PAGES   FIVE CENTS

VOLUME 92 — No. 161

DECEMBER 27, 1952

"I SAW MOMMY KISSING SANTA CLAUS" SUNG BY JIMMY BOYD IS THE NO. 1 HIT SINGLE

Christmas dreams came true when that most-anticipated gift was unwrapped.

Kiddies Victrola phonographs that played 45 rpm records were purchased as gifts.

The Toni Play-Wave doll's hair could be washed and permanently waved.

SPACE ACADEMY

Imaginations were stimulated by this "Tom Corbett" Space Academy play set, complete with rocket ships, flying saucers, radar and figures in space suits.

HELP MAKE THEIR DREAMS COME TRUE

Toni PLAY WAVE

FAMOUS BIRTHDAYS
Cathy Rigby-McCoy, December 12
Olympic gymnast and actress
June Anderson, December 30
soprano

The Saturday Evening
POST
January 19, 1952 - 15¢
THE FULL STORY OF
THE HOLLYWOOD-TV FIGHT
By Milton MacKaye
THE NORTHLAKE OUTRAGE
A Report on a Shocking Chicago Crime
By John Bartlow Martin
Some indeed among us are not so much griev'd for the present State of our Affairs, as apprehensive for the future. They observe, that no Revenue is sufficient without Economy, and that the most plentiful Income of a whole People from the natural Productions of their Country may be dissipated in vain and needless Expences, and Poverty be introduced in the place of Affluence.
Benj. Franklin

More *The Saturday Evening Post* Covers

The Saturday Evening Post covers were works of art, many illustrated by famous artists of the time, including Norman Rockwell. Most of the 1952 covers have been incorporated within the previous pages of this book; the few that were not are presented on the following pages for your enjoyment.

The Saturday Evening
POST
February 9, 1952 - 15¢
IN THIS ISSUE
One of the Great Books of Our Time:
WHITTAKER CHAMBERS'
OWN STORY OF THE
HISS CASE
A story that, for the first time, will show you the true dimensions of the communist threat to America

The Saturday Evening
POST
March 8, 1952 - 15¢
Did They Really Solve
The Lindbergh Case?
By CRAIG THOMPSON
Why Did Hiss Think He
Could Get Away With It?
By WHITTAKER CHAMBERS

The Saturday Evening

POST

August 23, 1952 · 15¢

THE CURIOUS CASE OF THE PRESIDENT'S BATHTUB
By Beverly Smith

THE HUNT FOR NEW METALS:
They're Finding Fortunes in the Hills

JOHN FALTER

The Saturday Evening

POST

October 25, 1952 – 15¢

THE INSIDE STORY OF OUR FIRST HYDROGEN BOMB
By Stewart Alsop and Dr. Ralph Lapp

The Saturday Evening

POST

November 15, 1952 · 15¢

The Whittaker Chambers I Know
By CRAIG THOMPSON

THE BLIND PASTOR OF MANHATTAN

The Saturday Evening

POST

November 29, 1952 – 15¢

The Nine Lives of a Parachute Tester
By VICTOR BOESEN

HERB SHRINER:
Shrewd Bumpkin of Television
By PETER ORDWAY

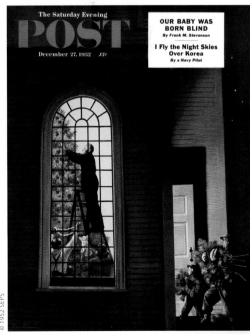

The Saturday Evening

POST

December 27, 1952 15¢

OUR BABY WAS BORN BLIND
By Frank M. Stevenson

I Fly the Night Skies Over Korea
By a Navy Pilot

MORE FAMOUS BIRTHDAYS

January 3
Jim Ross, wrestling announcer

January 14
Maureen Dowd, journalist

January 15
Melvyn Gale, English-born cellist (Electric Light Orchestra)

January 20
Paul Stanley, guitarist, singer, and musician (Kiss)

January 21
Louis Menand, writer and critic

January 29
Tommy Ramone, record producer and musician (The Ramones)

February 1
Stan Kasten, baseball executive

February 4
Jerry Shirley, rock drummer (Humble Pie)

February 10
Mike Varty, professional football player

February 12
Michael McDonald, singer and songwriter (The Doobie Brothers)

February 19
Amy Tan, novelist

February 22
William Frist, politician and heart surgeon

February 23
Brad Whitford, rhythm guitarist (Aerosmith)

February 24
Maxine Chernoff, poet, novelist and editor

February 29
Tim Powers, fantasy author

March 1
Alice Ritzman, professional golfer

March 4
Ron Moss, actor

March 11
Douglas Adams, science fiction author

March 19
Harvey Weinstein, producer

March 22
Bob Costas, sports announcer

March 23
Kim Stanley Robinson, author

March 29
Teófilo Stevenson, Cuban boxer

March 31
Vanessa del Rio, actress

April 4
Gary Moore, musician, songwriter, and producer (Skid Row and Thin Lizzy)

April 5
Mitch Pileggi, actor

April 6
Marilu Henner, actress and author

April 12
Ralph Wiley, sports journalist

April 15
Sam McMurray, actor

April 16
Bill Belicheck, football coach
Billy West, voice actor

April 26
Spice Williams-Crosby, actress and stunt performer

April 27
George Gervin, basketball player

May 6
Gregg Henry, actor and musician
Michael O'Hare, actor

May 11
Mike Lupica, sports journalist
Frances Fisher, British-born actress
Renaud, composer

May 14
Robert Zemeckis, film director
David Byrne, musician and songwriter (Talking Heads)

May 18
George Strait, country musician
Diane Duane, writer

May 19
Barbara Joyce Lomas, vocalist (B.T. Express)

May 26
David Meece, Christian musician

May 28
Victoria Cunningham, actress

June 4
Scott Wesley Brown, Christian musician

June 5
Nicko McBrain, musician (Iron Maiden)

June 7
Liam Neeson, Irish actor

June 11
Donnie Van Zant, rock vocalist and guitarist (38 Special)

June 12
Junior Brown, singer

June 16
Gino Vannelli, singer

June 17
Mike Milbury, ice hockey player, coach and executive

June 18
Carol Kane, actress
Isabella Rossellini, Italian actress

June 27
Douglas Unger, novelist

July 5
Terence T. Henricks, astronaut

July 12
Philip Taylor Kramer, rock musician

July 14
Franklin Graham, evangelist
Stan Shaw, actor

July 15
Terry O'Quinn, actor
David Pack, musician and producer

July 16
Stewart Copeland, rock musician

July 17
Phoebe Snow, singer
Nicolette Larson, singer
David Hasselhoff, actor

July 19
Allen Collins, rock musician (Lynyrd Skynyrd)

July 24
Gus Van Sant, film director

July 31
Chris Ahrens, ice hockey player

August 6
Pat MacDonald, singer-songwriter and musician
  (Timbuk 3)

August 9
Vicki Morgan, model

August 10
Daniel Hugh Kelly, actor

August 13
Herb Ritts, photographer

August 16
Reginald VelJohnson, actor

August 19
Jonathan Frakes, actor and director

August 20
John Hiatt, singer

August 27
Paul Reubens, actor, writer and comedian
Laurie Wisefield, guitarist for Wishbone Ash

August 28
Rita Dove, Pulitzer Prize winner in poetry

September 9
Angela Cartwright, child actress, photographer
  and painter

September 12
Gerry Beckley, singer and songwriter (America)

September 13
Randy Jones, disco and pop singer
  (The Village People)

September 19
Nile Rodgers, musician, composer and guitarist
  (The Honeydrippers)

September 22
Bob Goodlatte, politician

September 23
Jim Morrison, baseball player

September 24
Joseph Patrick Kennedy II, son of Robert F.
  Kennedy and Ethel Skakel Kennedy

September 25
Tommy Norden, actor
Jimmy Garvin, professional wrestler

September 29
Max Sandlin, politician

September 30
Jack Wild, English actor

October 7
Mary Badham, actress

October 9
Sharon Osbourne, British-born wife and
  manager of Ozzy Osbourne

October 14
Harry Anderson, actor and magician

October 16
Ron Taylor, actor

October 21
Patti Davis, daughter of President Ronald and
  Mrs. (Nancy Davis) Reagan

October 22
Jeff Goldblum, actor

November 2
Maxine Nightingale, singer
Alan Winstanley, producer

November 6
Michael Cunningham, writer

November 7
David Petraeus, general

November 8
Alfre Woodard, actress

November 11
Paul Cowsill, musician (The Cowsills)

November 15
Randy Savage, professional wrestler

November 16
Roger Bisby, English journalist

November 27
James D. Wetherbee, astronaut

November 28
S. Epatha Merkerson, actress

November 30
Keith Giffen, comic book writer and artist
Semyon Bychkov, conductor

December 3
Don Barnes, rock vocalist and guitarist (38
  Special)

December 7
Susan Collins, politician

December 12
Sarah Douglas, English actress

December 15
Julie Taymor, film, theater, and opera director and
  costume designer

December 27
David Knopfler, singer-songwriter, guitarist and
  pianist (Dire Straits)

Facts and Figures of 1952

President of the U.S.
Harry S. Truman
Vice President of the U.S.
Alben W. Barkley

Population of the U.S.
157,552,740

Births
3,913,000

High School Graduates
Males: 569,000
Females: 627,000

Average Salary for Full-Time Employee: $3,658.00
Minimum Wage (per hour): $0.75
Unemployment Rate: 3.0%
Rate of Inflation: 2.29%

U.S. NAVY, COURTESY OF HARRY S. TRUMAN LIBRARY

Average cost for:

Bread (lb.)...............................$0.16

Bacon (lb.)............................$0.65

Butter (lb.)............................$0.86

Eggs (doz.)...........................$0.67

Milk (½ gal.).........................$0.48

Potatoes (10 lbs.)................$0.76

Coffee (lb.)..........................$0.87

Sugar (5 lb.).........................$0.52

Gasoline (gal.)......................$0.20

Movie Ticket.........................$0.60

Postage Stamp.....................$0.03

New home.....................$9,050.00

REPRINTED WITH PERMISSION FROM HONEYWELL INTERNATIONAL

REPRINTED WITH PERMISSION FROM FORD MOTOR COMPANY

Notable Inventions and Firsts

January 10: Cecil B. DeMille's circus epic, *The Greatest Show on Earth*, premieres at Radio City Music Hall in New York City.

March 20: The United States Senate ratifies a peace treaty with Japan.

March 21: Alan Freed presents Moondog Coronation Ball at old Cleveland Arena and 25,000 attend first rock 'n' roll concert ever.

April 28: Treaty of San Francisco goes into effect, formally ending the war between Japan and the Allies.

June 30: *The Guiding Light* premieres on CBS and later becomes one of the longest running day-time soap operas on television.

September 20: The first commercial UHF television station in the world KPTV begins broadcasting in Portland, Ore.

September 30: The Cinerama widescreen system, invented by Fred Waller, debuts with the film *This Is Cinerama*.

REPRINTED WITH PERMISSION FROM FORD MOTOR COMPANY

October 30: Clarence Birdseye sells first frozen peas.

November: Kellogg's Frosted Flakes introduced, along with its famous pitch character, Tony the Tiger, and his tag line "They're G-g-g-great!"

December 14: The first successful surgical separation of Siamese twins is conducted in Mount Sinai Hospital in Cleveland, Ohio.

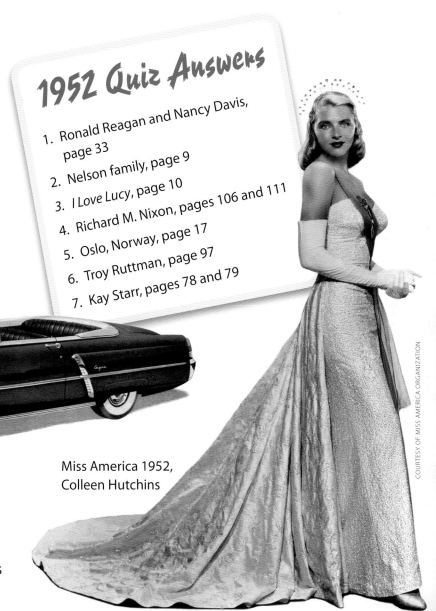

1952 Quiz Answers

1. Ronald Reagan and Nancy Davis, page 33
2. Nelson family, page 9
3. *I Love Lucy*, page 10
4. Richard M. Nixon, pages 106 and 111
5. Oslo, Norway, page 17
6. Troy Ruttman, page 97
7. Kay Starr, pages 78 and 79

Miss America 1952, Colleen Hutchins

COURTESY OF MISS AMERICA ORGANIZATION

Sports Winners
NFL: Detroit Lions defeat Cleveland Browns
NBA: Minneapolis Lakers defeat Syracuse Nationals
World Series: New York Yankees defeat Brooklyn Dodgers
Stanley Cup: Detroit Red Wings defeat Montreal Canadiens
The Masters: Sam Snead wins
PGA Championship: Jim Turnesa wins

Live It Again 1952

PROJECT EDITOR	Barb Sprunger
ART DIRECTOR	Brad Snow
COPYWRITER	Becky Sarasin
COPY SUPERVISOR	Deborah Morgan
PRODUCTION ARTIST SUPERVISOR	Erin Augsburger
PRODUCTION ARTIST	Edith Teegarden
COPY EDITOR	Emily Carter
PHOTOGRAPHY SUPERVISOR	Tammy Christian
NOSTALGIA EDITOR	Ken Tate
EDITORIAL DIRECTOR	Jeanne Stauffer
PUBLISHING SERVICES DIRECTOR	Brenda Gallmeyer

Printed in China
First Printing: 2011
Library of Congress Control Number: 2011922425
ISBN: 978-1-59217-348-8

Customer Service
LiveItAgain.com
(800) 829-5865

1 2 3 4 5 6 7 8 9